COLONIAL PEOPLE

The Wheelwright

CHRISTINE PETERSEN

Cavendish Square

New York

Published in 2014 by Cavendish Square Publishing, LLC
303 Park Avenue South, Suite 1247, New York, NY 10010

Copyright © 2014 by Cavendish Square Publishing, LLC

First Edition

CPSIA Compliance Information: Batch #WS13CSQ

All websites were available and accurate when this book was sent to press.

Library of Congress Cataloging-in-Publication Data

Petersen, Christine.
The wheelwright / Christine Petersen.
p. cm. — (Colonial people)
Includes bibliographical references and index.
Summary: "Explores the life of a colonial wheelwright and his importance to the community, as well as everyday life responsibilities, and social practices during that time"—Provided by publisher.
ISBN 978-1-60870-419-4 (hardcover) — ISBN 978-1-62712-049-4 (paperback) — ISBN 978-1-60870-988-5 (ebook)
1. Wheelwrights—United States—History—17th century—Juvenile literature. 2. Wheelwrights—United States—History—18th century—Juvenile literature. 3. Carriage and wagon making—United States—History—17th century—Juvenile literature. 4. Carriage and wagon making—United States—History—18th century—Juvenile literature. 5. United States—Social life and customs—To 1775—Juvenile literature. 6. United States—History—Colonial period, ca. 1600-1775—Juvenile literature. I. Title. II. Series.
HD8039.C332U66 2013
331.7'6886—dc23
2011028345

Editor: Peter Mavrikis
Art Director: Anahid Hamparian
Series Designer: Kay Petronio

Expert Reader: Paul Douglas Newman, Ph.D., Department of History, University of Pittsburgh at Johnstown

Photo research by Marybeth Kavanagh

Cover photo by Mary Evans Picture Library/The Image Works

The photographs in this book are used by permission and through the courtesy of: *SuperStock:* 4; *North Wind Picture Archives:* 7, 16, 20, 22, 33, 36; *The Image Works:* Lee Snider, 8; akg-images, 10, 11; Mary Evans, 18; Market Photos/HIP, 29; *The Colonial Williamsburg Foundation:* 14; *Getty Images:* Hulton Archive, 26; The Granger Collection, NYC: 31, 38; *The Art Archive:* Museo della Civilta Romana Rome/Gianni Dagli Orti, 30

Printed in the United States of America

CONTENTS

ONE

Colonists on the Move

English settlers began to establish permanent colonies on the Atlantic Coast of North America in the first decades of the seventeenth century. Their small communities were tucked along the Chesapeake and Massachusetts bays and near major rivers such as the James, Connecticut, and Susquehanna.

Settlers had several reasons for living near water. Over the centuries, American Indians had cleared trees along the Atlantic shoreline to make room for their own villages and farms. It was convenient to build colonial settlements on cleared land that was not in use by local Indian tribes. Just inland lay dense forests, which seemed to go on forever. English colonists were used to cities, or to the park-like countryside of England where most forests had been cut down decades earlier. They not only found it difficult to travel through American forests, but also felt fearful

After landing on the banks of Virginia's James River,
English colonists give thanks for a safe journey and
the rich land that they hope to settle.

of these wild places when it was necessary to enter. The ocean and rivers provided a bounty of food, and were good routes for transportation. When possible, colonists stuck to the water and avoided the forests.

By the 1630s newly arriving colonists had begun to spread away from the original settlements in search of farmland. In the south, Virginia's hilly landscape was crisscrossed with small streams and rivers that rushed downhill toward the sea. Low spots in the land trapped water, forming marshes that were almost impassable. Settlers searched out pockets of land with the best soil, usually alongside streams. To overcome their isolation, they established footpaths between farms and learned to build Indian-style canoes. These were perfect for paddling up- and downstream to visit other farms and the nearest village. Canoes were fragile, however, so southern farmers also constructed flat-bottomed boats. These were used to transport heavy barrels of tobacco, which quickly became the South's most important crop. On the return trip they could be loaded with goods purchased from village **craftsmen** or the local general store.

Massachusetts lay hundreds of miles north of Virginia. This area was not so hilly but also contained deep forests, fast

Colonists and local American Indian tribes often traded goods and food.

streams, and soggy marshes. Colonists here were deeply religious Congregationalists, sometimes known as Pilgrims or Puritans. They were also farmers, but they valued community and chose to live in tight-knit villages with farm fields around the edges. These colonists found that American Indians had already established a network of trails in their area. These **traces** wound along the coastline and through patches of forest. Indians walked in single file so the traces were rarely more than a foot wide, but they became deep after long use. Traces soon widened from the passage of colonists, who walked in groups or with cattle and other livestock. The traces continued to change and grow larger as wealthier colonists began to **import** horses from England.

In 1639 the Massachusetts General Court ordered that a formal road be built so residents of coastal villages could more easily reach Boston. This port town had become an important

This reconstruction shows how Plymouth Plantation may have looked soon after its settlement in 1620.

destination for many northern travelers. The road began at the shipbuilding village of Newport and extended south as far as Plymouth. Land surveyors were hired to do the work. The Massachusetts colonial government allowed them to put the road wherever it would "bee most convenient so as it occation not the puling down of any man's house or laying open any garden or orchard."

As in Virginia, some colonists from Massachusetts moved inland. They heard rumors of excellent farmland to the west, along the Connecticut River where a small group of Dutch colonists had recently settled. In the seventeenth century there was no road to this place. Families packed up their belongings and slung them over the backs of oxen and horses. It took them days to reach the river by following Indian trails. They sometimes had to chop down trees and brush to widen the path. Rushing streams threatened to sweep livestock and belongings away when the travelers crossed. Despite the challenges, this was only the first of many such migrations.

This steady flow of people to America was part of England's effort to set up colonies located around the world. In this **imperial** system, the English put native peoples, colonists, and imported slaves to work collecting valuable natural

Colonists spent much of their time collecting natural resources that were shipped back to England.

resources from each colony. These materials were shipped back to England where English craftsmen manufactured them into products. Wagons, and the wheelwrights who made them, were essential to make this system work. Raw materials such as metal, wood, and leather were loaded into wagons and transported to the coasts for shipment to England. Finished goods were shipped back to the colonies and carried by wagon to distant villages. Although made from American materials, the products were sold to colonists at high prices that profited the English merchants and government. It was part of an unfair system that eventually led colonists to seek their independence.

On the Road

Throughout the seventeenth century and into the eighteenth, English settlers continued to arrive in America. More came from

By the mid-eighteenth century, Philadelphia had become one of the largest and most elegant cities on the colonial Atlantic coastline.

Ireland, Germany, and other parts of Europe. Ships deposited the immigrants in port cities such as Philadelphia, Boston, and New York. The desire for land drove them north, south, and west. New colonies were established, and communities formed wherever land was offered.

By 1700 more than 250,000 people lived in colonial America. Their numbers would continue to increase, yet many farms and villages remained isolated. With no coastline or rivers nearby, these communities had no easy way to transport goods or communicate with each other. It took as long as a week for travelers to cover even 100 miles on foot or horseback. Cargo had to be packed on the backs of horses or piled onto sledges and dragged across the ground. These slow and dangerous methods resulted in many injuries and damaged goods. England's growing imperial economy demanded a more efficient system of transportation.

The solution was an improved system of roads that would extend outward from major cities into distant parts of the countryside. This was a big undertaking. The English government took no interest in roads and offered no money to assist. Colonies that wanted roads had to raise the money themselves, usually by requiring residents to pay a special tax.

Some colonies used tax money to hire road workers who not only built but also maintained the roads. In other regions colonists were expected to pitch in with their time and strength as well as their pocketbooks. A Georgia law written in 1755 required adult male colonists to work on roads as many as twelve days a year. Those who avoided this duty were fined.

In most cases colonial roads were simply wide dirt tracks around which the trees had been cut. Still, this was an improvement over traces and trails because it allowed travelers to walk or ride in large groups and see clearly for long distances. Even with care these roads became potholed and muddy. In the eighteenth century some regions chose to lay wooden planks or logs over frequently used sections of road.

Roads typically circled around marshes to avoid the gooey mud and thick plant growth. Some streams were shallow enough for travelers to plow across, but deep, fast-flowing rivers required a more permanent solution. Building bridges took even more manpower and money than laying a long section of road. Where colonists could cross on foot, they might simply fell a tree to serve as a bridge. On busier roads, ferries were installed. These flat rafts could hold a lot of weight and were pushed across the water with poles or pulled by a rope.

Roads often crossed private property. Some landowners and clever businessmen got the idea to set up **turnpikes**. They constructed and kept the roads with no help (or interference) from the government. The owners happily allowed others to use their "pikes," but there was a catch. The roads were blocked at intervals and travelers had to pay a fee before continuing along the way.

The Value of Vehicles

It was not enough to have more and better roads. Colonists also needed sturdy, wheeled vehicles that could carry large loads over

Coachmakers in Colonial Williamsburg prepare a carriage for travel.

them. The skilled craftsmen who made these vehicles were called wheelwrights.

The arrival of wheeled vehicles in America was an important technological step. It allowed colonists to do more work at a faster pace. A farmer could hitch a two-wheeled **cart** to his horse or ox. He loaded it with produce to sell at market or moved large bags of grain to the flour mill. Tobacco, timber, and furs were the colonies' most valuable **exports**, but most of these goods were collected inland. Large **wagons**, pulled by several horses, carried them to distant port cities for shipment to England. Wagons returned to the countryside loaded with merchandise that colonists had purchased from the home country. Other types of heavy **freight**, such as iron, hay, and firewood, were transported locally or between colonies in wagons.

Colonists were also eager to be in touch with each other. Wagons were eventually used to distribute mail and carry people around the countryside. Military troops and supplies moved in wagon trains along colonial roads as well. This flow of goods, people, and information made the growing country feel more unified. Eventually, it contributed to the colonies' sense of independence from England.

King of the Wagons

Pennsylvania wheelwrights became famous for developing a large type of wagon called the Conestoga. It had four wheels like other wagons but was both larger and sturdier. The Conestoga's body dipped gently in the middle and its sidewalls were exceptionally high. The sides angled outward, allowing the cargo to shift rather than fall out when the wagon leaned on a curve or hill. Also important were the Conestoga's wheels. Their large size kept cargo high and dry when the wagon was driven across streams and mud puddles. Unique to the Conestoga wagon was a set of wooden hoops that arched over the body. These were fixed to the outside of the wainscoting. A driver might normally leave the hoops exposed, but in bad weather he could draw a tightly fitting cloth cover across them to protect the goods in his wagon.

TWO

Wheels for the People

In colonial America, everything was made by hand. The blacksmith manufactured and mended iron tools. Carpenters constructed buildings. Tailors and shoemakers made clothing, while the apothecary provided medicines. Larger towns were home to many different craftsmen, each providing some essential service.

The wheelwright also became an important worker in colonial America, but not for almost a century after the first settlement took place. Colonists may have built simple wheelbarrow-type carts or imported them from England in the seventeenth century. Yet the first wheeled vehicles did not appear in colonial communities until the late 1600s. These small **chaises** had two wide wheels and a seat large enough to hold two people. Atop the long, bench-like seat stretched a leather or linen awning,

The wheelwright often worked in a large shop, side by side with other craftsmen who built colonial vehicles.

which might be folded down on clear days. Long wooden poles extended parallel to each wheel and were strapped to the leather harness worn by a single horse. The chaise did not offer a comfortable ride—but what a convenience to roll through the city streets, remaining clean and dry while others walked! The owners of chaises were colonial gentlemen, who imported the vehicles from England to show off their wealth.

Working Vehicles

Chaises might have caught colonists' attention, but their use was slow to catch on. This was especially true in New England, where Congregationalists considered pride and laziness to be sins. More practical were freight vehicles, which could transport cargo around the farm, through the city, or to distant locations. At first, colonists imported wheels from England and built carts and wagons to go with them. By the early 1700s colonial wheelwrights had begun to make wheels locally, fitting them on carts and wagons of many styles and sizes.

A cart typically sat on two wheels like a chaise and could be pulled by one or two horses. Wagons were larger, requiring four wheels and a team of four to six horses. A thick wooden **shaft** joined each pair of wheels so that they rolled together. Flexible leather straps or thin strips of hickory wood attached the shafts to a larger frame, which supported the body. The leather and hickory acted like springs, allowing the body to bounce rather than jolt over bumps in the road.

All carts and wagons had wooden sidewalls, or wainscoting, to hold in their cargo. The wheelwright usually built a gate at the back of the vehicle. He might add a ramp that sloped down to the ground. Workers could roll even the heaviest barrels along

Wagons could hold heavy loads because they were pulled by teams of strong animals such as oxen or horses.

this ramp or walk cargo directly into the body. Some wagons were permanently attached to only one set of wheels. A wooden pin could be used to connect the wagon to a second set of wheels. When this was removed, the cart tipped up and its cargo was easy to remove.

Another part of the vehicle's frame was a long pole that extended toward the front. Horses wore leather harnesses and oxen were fitted with wooden neck yokes. The animals were lined up on either side of the pole and hitched to it. When the driver hollered "Hip!" they walked forward, pulling the vehicle behind. A call of "Gee!" and a tug on the reins sent them to the right, and "Haw!" caused the animals to turn left. Their motion shifted the pole, turning the wheels and the cart with them. On the farm, all hands were needed during the harvest. Boys learned to drive from a young age, and it was not uncommon to see a woman at the reins of a vehicle.

Many Uses

A farmer or carpenter might learn to make a decent wagon body. But it took a wheelwright's skill and experience to build good wheels. He manufactured them for the freight vehicles constructed in his own shop. The wheelwright also sold wheels to coach makers, who made chaises and other passenger vehicles. Another important part of the wheelwright's job was to repair wheels imported from England.

Transportation was not the only purpose for wheels in colonial America. Wheels were often used in machines because they made work easier or faster. Some of these machines were manufactured in England and imported, but the wheelwright could make them when his customers asked.

A spinning wheel was found in almost every home in the

colonial countryside. Used by women to make yarn, its design was fairly simple. A large wheel sat atop a wooden frame. A narrow belt ran over its **rim** to a much smaller pulley. The user spun a handle on the wheel with one hand. The wheel spun a belt, which turned the pulley. Before she began to spin, the woman attached a bit of wool or plant fiber to a cylindrical bobbin mounted beside the pulley. With her free hand, she continued to drag out narrow lengths of this material from a pile at her feet as she turned the wheel. The fiber wrapped around a bobbin, forming tidy threads

The spinning wheel was constructed much like a vehicle wheel.

Right of Way

As traffic increased on colonial roads, there was greater need for drivers to show caution and share a similar set of rules to prevent accidents. Colonial governments did not create such rules until the 1790s, so colonists began to adopt them independently. The easiest rule to follow was right of way. This ensured that vehicles going in the same direction stayed on one side of the road, leaving room for those traveling the opposite way to pass.

English drivers had always chosen the left side of the road. Perhaps because most people are right-handed, colonists opted to drive on the right. The wheelwright built Conestoga wagons to accommodate this choice. It was designed so that the driver could sit on the left side of the vehicle. If he drove on the right, this placed him closest to the middle of the road—the location with the best view for safety. The brake on the Conestoga was also placed on the left. His right hand was then free to handle the reins, which controlled a team of two or more horses or oxen. The Conestoga also had a small running board on the left side where a driver could stand and keep an eye on the road. Alternatively, he rode on the left-hand horse closest to the wagon. Even colonists who walked or rode on horseback obeyed this informal rule and kept to the "right of way."

of yarn. When the bobbin was full, it could be removed and sold to weavers who made cloth, or saved for home sewing projects.

Woodworkers used a similar wheel on a tool called the great wheel lathe. As much as 6 feet tall, this carpenter's wheel might be mounted on a frame or on the wall. As with the spinning wheel, its belt ran to a pulley. The carpenter fitted a piece of wood between two posts next to the pulley. The ends of the wood hooked into pins that rotated with the pulley. An assistant turned a handle on the wheel while the carpenter held a chisel or other sharp tool to the piece of wood. Shavings peeled off wherever the chisel was placed, forming patterns that encircled the wood. The great wheel lathe was ideal for making table legs and similar objects that required a round or ornately carved shape.

Both of these wheels had a similar design, with a central **hub** bearing **spokes** that radiated out toward a circular rim. Gears were a totally different type of wheel. Made of solid wood, they had notches cut into their edges or pegs hammered along the sides. When two gears were placed side by side, their notches or pegs interlocked. The motion of one gear caused the other to turn. Gears were part of the machinery in mills, which were among the most important colonial industries. Mills were built in most communities to grind grain and cut lumber for construction.

THREE

Building a Wheel

It took many years for the wheelwright to learn the skills necessary to make wagons, carts, and the variety of wheels used in colonial America. His training usually began in late childhood. An experienced wheelwright trained his son but also took on **apprentices**. These were boys from the community whose fathers signed a contract requesting the craftsman to teach them. The master wheelwright promised to look after a boy, providing housing and food. Over a period of years he would pass on his knowledge of the wheelwright trade. The master was also expected to make sure his apprentice got a general education, learning to read, write, and do math. These skills would help the boy become a good citizen and businessman.

Like a student in school, the apprentice received no wages for his long hours and hard work. The master had the right to

Making wheels was hard physical work that required both strength and patience.

punish an apprentice who was disrespectful or lazy. The reward for the apprentice's hard work was knowledge and a set of skills to help him earn a living. At the end of his training a young man was called a **journeyman**. He received a set of tools and was ready to be hired. Eventually he might acquire the skills and save enough money to open his own shop, becoming a master wheelwright like his teacher.

The Heart of the Wheel

Long before he could make a vehicle, the wheelwright had to find the perfect wood. He usually visited the forest, choosing the trees he liked rather than purchasing lumber from a sawmill. After the trees were cut, logs were brought to the wheelwright's shop and cut into boards about the same size as particular parts of wheels and vehicles. They were stacked in a storage shed and left to dry, sometimes for years. The wheelwright could not rush this part of the process. Moisture made the boards warp, and bent wood was hard to work with.

The wheel contained several parts. The wheelwright began at its center, by making the hub. This part of the wheel connected to the shafts and frame of the vehicle, which held up the body. It would have to support a lot of weight. The wheelwright chose a rectangular block of gum or elm. These were extremely hard woods and rarely split. He placed the block on a great wheel lathe identical to the kind employed by carpenters, and carved it to create a barrel shape. The wheelwright hollowed a tunnel through the length of the hub and lined it with an iron tube. One end of the shaft would slip through this space. The iron tube allowed the wheel to spin freely around the shaft. The end of the shaft would project slightly beyond the hub. At its tip was a wooden pin that kept the wheel steady on the shaft. When the wheelwright or driver needed to remove the wheel from the vehicle, he had only to take out this pin.

The wheelwright also bound the hub's outer ends with iron bands to strengthen the wood. He then cut a series of **mortises** around the curved outer edge of the hub. One spoke would fit into each of these slots. Oak was the wood of choice for spokes. This type of wood could withstand bumpy colonial roads but provided a little bounce rather than stiffness. The apprentice learned to shape spokes, rounding the edges and making one end thinner so it would slip into the mortise.

Spokes and Rim

Spokes were fairly simple to make, but their position on the hub was crucial. Each spoke was set at a slight angle rather than perpendicular to the hub. This gave the finished wheel a slightly dished shape. As the wheel turned, spokes at the bottom stood vertically while those at the top bent away from the body of the vehicle. This supported the vehicle while providing room for its body to sway from side to side as the animals pulling it plodded down the road.

The wheel was constructed of several parts that fit together seamlessly.

The wheel rim was made of several curved sections called **felloes**. The wheelwright kept patterns from which felloes were cut, but the apprentice needed practice choosing the correct one. This depended on the size of the wheel. It might take half a dozen felloes to form the rim circle, and their curvature had to be just right. This was done with an **adze**, a tool similar to an axe but with a curved blade. When the felloes had been cut, they were smoothed with a rectangular wooden tool called a **plane**. A hollow in the center of the plane held a blade, which had a wedge of wood on top to keep it from slipping. The apprentice

Invention of the Wheel

The oldest known wheels were made in Mesopotamia, a region that was located between the Tigris and Euphrates rivers (now in the nations of Iraq and Syria). Circular stone rings have been found in this area that were built approximately 5,500 years ago. These were not designed for transportation, but for making pottery. Ancient craftsmen lay their wheels atop a wooden or stone platform and spun them to reach all sides of a piece of clay as they worked.

It took several more centuries for people to realize that wheels could also be used for transportation. The invention of wheeled vehicles came in stages. Ancient people first tried laying down logs and rolling heavy objects atop them. They later built sledges with skate-like runners that could slide across the ground. The sledge rolled faster when it was pulled across a path of logs. But this required the logs to be moved constantly in front of the sledge. The next step was to build a sledge with logs on the bottom. Held inside frames, they could roll freely but carried the sledge with them. Fine-tuning of this design resulted in a thin shaft with large, solid wheels at each end. This shaft was attached to the body of the vehicle—now a cart. By 2000 BCE the solid wheel had been replaced by one with spokes. This reduced the weight of the wheel and cart, making it easier to maneuver.

learned to hold this tool carefully, one hand on each end, and scrape it over the surface of the wood.

After a felloe had been leveled, mortises were cut into its curved inner surface to hold two spokes. The wheelwright gradually hammered each felloe onto its pair of spokes. He kept hammering until all the felloes fit together, forming a perfect circle.

A local blacksmith forged strips of iron to cover the rim. These **strakes** were curved like the felloes and about the same length. The wheelwright positioned each strake so it fit over a joint between two felloes. This reduced the risk that the wooden parts of the wheel's rim would separate. The result was an iron tire that protected the wheelwright's fine wooden wheel from wear and tear on the road. The wheel could now be mounted on a vehicle. It was ready to roll.

Different tools were used for each step of wheel construction.

FOUR

Moving West

By the mid-eighteenth century, the creak and groan of rolling wagon wheels had become a familiar sound to colonists' ears. Wheelwrights had plenty of business, especially if they made big Conestoga wagons. Most Conestogas were built in southeastern Pennsylvania, in or around Lancaster. In 1770, this town was home to five master wheelwrights. More than two dozen blacksmiths and woodworkers also worked in Lancaster's wagon manufacturing industry.

These men did not work alone. In addition to apprentices, wheelwrights and other colonial craftsmen often kept servants and slaves. Some servants were poor people who had been eager to come to America because they heard that it was possible to obtain land. In England and Europe, land was available only to the wealthy. Willing to do whatever it took for such a great reward, poor people might agree to sign a contract called an **indenture**. A wealthy landowner, craftsman, or businessman paid their fare to America. They became servants, required to work for several years to pay back the debt. Other people had no choice about coming to the colonies. They were rounded up from prisons and poorhouses and put on boats. However they arrived, only a small percentage of indentured servants survived to earn their land. Servitude was difficult work, and many indentured servants died of exhaustion or disease.

The wheelwright found it helpful to have extra workers in his shop. But like apprentices, the indentured

A Conestoga wagon traveling the Wilderness Road across the Appalachian Mountains.

servants who survived eventually left. Some colonists considered it more advantageous to purchase slaves. This was particularly common in the South. In the eighteenth century, approximately 1.5 million slaves were brought to colonies in the Caribbean. Most had been kidnapped from West Africa. Approximately 250,000 of these people were transported northward and purchased by American colonists. The wheelwright might keep a few slaves, who did simple tasks around the shop or were trained in skilled work alongside his apprentices. He saw this as an investment, for the slave would remain with him or could be sold at any time. The owner spent very little on the care of a slave, providing only the most basic shelter and care. In return he received a lifetime of labor.

Fighting for the West

Conestoga wagons became the vehicle of choice for merchants shipping goods and for colonists moving inland. They were also used by military troops hauling supplies toward forts on the western frontier of the English colonies. When American patriots took up arms against the British in the Revolutionary War, Conestogas delivered weapons and food to battlefields throughout colonial America. Wheelwrights were never far from the action. They followed troops into battle and joined groups of colonists who struck out to settle the frontier.

Do Drop Inn

Even on the best roads, drivers could travel only so far before their horses became exhausted. Wagon drivers sometimes camped on the road. Families might do the same while moving to a new region. Yet this could be uncomfortable, and it was almost impossible during the winter months.

Colonists with homes near a road took pride in offering hospitality to travelers. They welcomed the company, which could provide a break from their otherwise routine lives. As traffic began to increase, some locals chose to set up taverns. These establishments offered a variety of services—food and drink, beds, a place to stable the horses, and sometimes entertainment. By the middle of the eighteenth century taverns (sometimes called inns) were spaced every 8 miles or so along the main colonial roads. To guarantee safe stops for wagon drivers and their goods, colonial governments began to build and maintain taverns. For this reason, taverns were sometimes called "public houses."

A tavern became the social hub of its community. But it was more than a place to learn the latest gossip. Tavernkeepers received and distributed mail, collected newspapers, and gathered news from passing travelers. Locals met to talk about important issues in colonial life and politics.

When a wagon wheel broke, travelers were grateful for the assistance of trained wheelwrights.

Travelers filled their Conestoga wagons with supplies in Lancaster and drove southwest on the Great Wagon Road into Virginia's Shenandoah Valley. There the Great Wagon Road joined an ancient American Indian trail that led southward into Georgia. After the year 1775, travelers had another choice. From the Shenandoah Valley they could cut west on the Wilderness Road. This led through a gap in the southern Appalachian

Mountains toward what is now Kentucky. This land had always been used as hunting grounds by Cherokee, Shawnee, and Iroquois Indian tribes. Here, as in other parts of colonial America, Indians were convinced and tricked into giving up their land, bit by bit. This region was not yet part of a colony in 1775, yet settlers flooded there to take a share of its rich soil.

Roads were also being built in the north, where fur traders and farmers began slipping west into the Ohio River Valley along the Forbes Road. The French had a long claim on this land and a comfortable relationship with its resident Indian tribes. They traded furs and explored, but they set up few permanent settlements. These new arrivals clearly had different intentions, and Indian tribes were nervous. Hundreds of soldiers arrived, cutting wide roads to make way for their huge Conestoga wagons. Settlers came through, making surprise attacks on Indian villages. For their part, the French wanted to avoid competition for fur supplies. In 1754 the two groups went to war—French and Indians against British and colonial troops. The prize was a huge expanse of land between the Appalachian Mountains and the Mississippi River.

The British won this war after nine years of ugly fighting, but the prize remained out of reach. Great Britain's King

George III and the country's Parliament passed a law called the Proclamation of 1763, ordering colonists to remain on the east side of the Appalachians. The British government wanted to establish a good relationship with the Indian tribes before settlers flooded in. But it also intended to keep colonists close together in the east for a while longer. Settlers who moved to the western frontier might become too independent, ignoring

Wheelwrights were among the valued craftsmen who joined thousands of settlers rolling west in wagon trains after the Revolutionary War.

colonial laws and making their own goods instead of buying those imported from Britain.

Many colonists resented being restricted to increasingly overcrowded eastern lands. They found it even more outrageous when Britain made new laws taxing them on printed and imported goods. Colonists knew that their tax money was being used to pay off Britain's debts after the French and Indian War. But they were not allowed a representative in the British Parliament to speak their concerns.

A steady trickle of settlers ignored these new laws and continued west. Others protested by refusing to buy imported goods or pay taxes. These patriots declared independence from the home country in 1776. Colonists became citizens of the United States of America after winning the Revolutionary War. Now they were free to move west. The wheelwright's unique skills would continue to be essential over the next century as the nation expanded toward the Pacific Ocean.

Make a Model Wheel

Your school or community arts center may have a woodworking shop where teachers can help you build a wooden wagon wheel. But you can test the construction of a wheel at home using simple materials from a craft shop. See how the parts fit together to form a dished wheel, then try it out. Race your wheel against a friend's, or develop your own design for a cart! This activity requires the use of sharp tools, so make sure you have an adult helper.

You Will Need

- a few sheets of newspaper
- Styrofoam bouquet ring (12-inch diameter with flat, not rounded, rim)
- Styrofoam disk arranger (4-inch diameter, with two flat sides and rounded rim)
- jumbo wooden craft sticks
- masking tape (1-inch width) or a glue gun
- duct or heavy-weight packing tape

- craft knife or other small knife
- scissors
- permanent marker
- ruler

OPTIONAL:
- wooden dowel (3/8-inch by 12-inch)
- rubber bands
- materials for a second complete wheel

Instructions

1. Spread the newspaper over a flat work surface. Lay the Styrofoam bouquet ring flat on the newspaper. Get your adult helper to cut the Styrofoam ring into two equal half-circles, using the craft knife. Cut these halves in half again. Refit these together as a circle and set aside.

2. Choose eight jumbo craft sticks. These are your "spokes." Measure a length of 4 inches from one end of a stick and mark this spot with your permanent marker. Use the scissors to cut the stick at this point. Repeat with the other sticks.

3. Lay the Styrofoam disk flat on your work surface. This will be your wheel's "hub," and you will insert the stick-spokes into its rounded edge. The position of the sticks is key to creating a dished wheel. There are three tricks to doing this correctly:

   a. The wide edges of the stick face the round side of the "hub."

   b. The stick should be placed closer to the bottom edge of the hub, not right at its center.

   c. Angle the stick very slightly upward. The free end (which you were holding) should be level with—but not above—the top of the disk.

4. Following the guidelines above, gently push the first stick into the disk. If you are dissatisfied with the angle of the stick-spoke, you can make small adjustments. Moving the stick too much will leave a large hole in the Styrofoam.

5. Insert the second stick on the opposite side of the disk. The others can be spaced equally between these on the disk, always in opposite pairs.

6. Place the four sections of your Styrofoam ring on the work surface around your spoked disk. These are your "felloes." Keeping the disk flat on your work surface, gently press one quarter-ring very slightly into two of the spokes. Fit the next section of the ring on the neighboring pair of spokes, and so on around the circle.

7. There will be space between the four sections of the ring. Close this up by pressing gently on each Styrofoam "felloe," then rotating the wheel

and doing the same around the circle. Repeat until the four pieces fit perfectly.

8. Loosen the pieces slightly and use a glue gun to seal the edges between felloes. Alternatively, small pieces of masking tape can be placed across the seams between sections of the wheel.

9. Cut four 9.5-inch sections of duct tape (or other heavy tape). These are the "strakes" to cover your wheel.

10. Place the first strake along the edge of the wheel. Center it to cover the joint between two felloes. Repeat with the other three pieces of tape. They should fit perfectly, end-to-end, around the wheel. You may have to trim the width of this "tire" to match your wheel. Now look at your wheel from the side. You should easily be able to see the dished shape of the spokes. Does your wheel roll well?

11. OPTIONAL: Add an axle to your wheel. Lay the wheel on a flat surface so that the "dish" faces downward. Press a wooden dowel (3/8 inch by 12 inch) through the center of the disk. Pick it up and push a little of the dowel out the far end of the disk-hub. Wrap a rubber band around both ends of the dowel to keep it from slipping. You can hold the dowel to spin the wheel in the air or on the ground.

12. Make a second wheel and use the dowel as a shaft, allowing the two wheels to turn together. Can you design and construct a cart to fit on your wheel assembly?

Glossary

adze	an axe-like tool with a curved blade
apprentice	a person who works with an expert to learn a new skill or job
cart	a two-wheeled vehicle pulled by horses or oxen
chaise	a two-wheeled passenger vehicle drawn by horses
craftsman	a trained worker who makes objects by hand
export	to sell to other regions or countries
felloe	one curved section of a wooden wheel
freight	goods transported from place to place
hub	the centerpiece of a wheel
imperial	describes the rule of one nation over a group of colonies or other nations
import	to buy from other regions or countries
indenture	a contract requiring a worker to serve an employer for some period of years
journeyman	a craftsman who has completed an apprenticeship
mortise	a hole in one object into which another piece is fitted
plane	a handheld tool used to smooth the surface of wood
rim	the circular outer edge of a wheel
shaft	a bar that connects two wheels
spoke	a bar that extends outward from a wheel's hub, supporting the rim

strake	an iron band fitted outside the wooden rim of a wheel
trace	a narrow path
turnpike	a road on which users are required to pay a toll
wagon	a four-wheeled vehicle pulled by horses or oxen
wainscoting	the wooden sidewalls of a cart or wagon

Find Out More

BOOKS

Kalman, Bobbie. *A Visual Dictionary of a Colonial Community.* New York: Crabtree Publishing Company, 2008.

Landau, Elaine. *Explore Jamestown with Elaine Landau.* Berkeley Heights, NJ: Enslow Elementary, 2006.

Love, Rebecca. *English Colonies in America.* Mankato, MN: Compass Point Books, 2008.

Thompson, Linda. *The First Settlements* (Expansion of America). Vero Beach, FL: Rourke Publishing, 2006.

WEBSITES

Carpentry Tools

http://www.history.org/foundation/journal/spring03/tools.cfm

Wheelwrights and carpenters used many similar tools. This site, from Colonial Williamsburg, provides drawings and descriptions of many common woodworking instruments.

Colonial Williamsburg Kids' Zone

http://www.history.org/kids/

Tour the colonial capital of Virginia and meet some of its important residents. There are games and activities, and many resources about colonial life and history.

The Conestoga Wagon

http://www.co.lancaster.pa.us/ lancastercity/cwp/ view.asp?A=3&Q=517058

Lancaster, Pennsylvania, was the home of the Conestoga wagon. Visit this site to see an authentic Conestoga and read a brief history of its role in colonial history.

The Wheelwright Trade

http://www.history.org/ Foundation/ journal/ Winter04-05/ wheelwright_ slideshow/

This slideshow provides a virtual tour of Colonial Williamsburg's wheelwright shop, showing workers and the tools they used.

Index

Page numbers in **boldface** are illustrations.

About the Author

Christine Petersen has enjoyed diverse careers as a bat biologist and middle school teacher. Now a freelance writer, she has published more than forty nonfiction books for children and young adults. In her free time, Petersen conducts naturalist programs near her Minnesota home and spends time with her young son. She is a member of the Society of Children's Book Writers and Illustrators.